# Xenophobe's®
guide to the
# ICELANDERS

## Richard Sale

Oval Books

Published by Oval Books,
London, UK

Telephone: +44 (0)20 7733 8585
E-mail: info@ovalbooks.com
Web site: www.ovalbooks.com

Published by Ravette Books, 1994

Published by Oval Books, 2000
Revised/updated 2001, 2003, 2005, 2007

New edition 2009, updated 2010

Editor – Catriona Tulloch Scott
Copy editor – Saffron Beatson
Series Editor – Anne Tauté

Cover designer – Vicki Towers
Printer – J. F. Print Ltd., Sparkford, Somerset
Producer – Oval Projects Ltd.

Acknowledgement and grateful thanks are given to:

Ruth Greenfield (www.ruthgreenfieldcards.com)
for the use of her photograph 'Reykjavík rooftops',
and the late William Jón Holm for the use of
his poem 'The Icelandic Language'.

Xenophobe's® is a Registered Trademark.

ISBN: 978-1-906042-36-3

# Contents

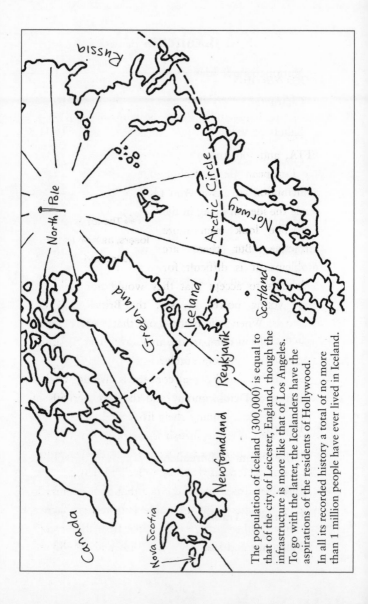

The population of Iceland (300,000) is equal to that of the city of Leicester, England, though the infrastructure is more like that of Los Angeles. To go with the latter, the Icelanders have the aspirations of the residents of Hollywood.

In all its recorded history a total of no more than 1 million people have ever lived in Iceland.

# Nationalism & Identity

## Forewarned

The Icelanders are Europeans, but only up to a point, the point lying about 200 miles offshore. They are members of the European Economic Area and of EFTA, and sometimes think they would like to join the European Union feeling that they have a huge contribution to make. And the global credit crunch made the idea of being in the Eurozone look even more attractive. But there are problems. It is difficult for

> **66** The Icelanders like losers, as long as they lose to Iceland that is. **99**

Icelanders to accept that they would not have the same voting power as, say, the British and the Germans. When it is pointed out that there are very few of them in comparison, they do not understand. One country, one vote, surely?

But the Icelanders' real concern is fishing. Cod is the basis of their economy and they are nervous of foreign trawlers ruining their livelihood. One of the reasons they like the British is because they lost the last Cod War. It was a friendly war and the Icelanders like losers, as long as they lose to Iceland that is.

Icelanders are proud of the fact that their country is unique. Nowhere else are there lava deserts, active volcanoes and icecaps. At the same time they recognise that as a nation they are tiny and of limited standing in the world. The insecurity this creates makes the Icelanders, a very close-knit nation with a developed sense of community, behave as though they were indeed the centre of the universe. It seems absolutely right to them that when Jules Verne sent his travellers to the centre of the earth, it was down through an Icelandic volcano.

> **66 To have the same roots as the Americans and even to share characteristics with the English was almost more than could be borne. 99**

In the winter of 1002/1003 Snorri Thorfinnsson was born in Vinland (nowadays believed to be either Newfoundland or Nova Scotia) of Icelandic parents, the first non-Indian American. It is only a matter of time before the Icelanders file a lawsuit claiming North America on behalf of Snorri's surviving relatives.

## How they see themselves

The Icelanders suffered a shock when a study of blood-types suggested that they might be of Gaelic, rather than Viking, stock. To have the same roots as the Americans (who are basically Irish and therefore quite beyond the pale), and even to share characteristics with the English (who are amiable enough but arrogant), was almost more than could be borne. As it was known (but kept very quiet) that when the Vikings arrived there were already Irish monks in Iceland, some historians suggested that there had actually been an Irish settlement and that the Vikings had either killed all the settlers or, much worse, interbred with them. It is now thought that the few monks who got there first left in disgust at having to share their sanctuary with heathens, and that the blood results could be explained away by natural causes or, better still, by the suggestion that the Vikings kidnapped a few Gaelic women from the Shetlands or Orkneys on the way. The national psyche has been restored to health.

Icelanders hold themselves in the very highest esteem. They are the sons of Vikings, the greatest of all ancient races, renowned for their strength, fortitude, good looks and masculine values. The fact that these same ancestors are also famous for pillage is discreetly ignored, as is their somewhat dubious attitude towards women. Icelanders are also reluctant to talk about Ingólfur, the first Viking to land on Iceland. As a mark of respect they have named the spot where he landed Ingólfshöfði, but they put it in small print on their maps so that as few people as possible notice that it is merely a knob of rock some three miles out to sea.

**66 As proof of their innate superiority Icelanders point out that Iceland is the navel of the world. 99**

As proof of their innate superiority Icelanders point out that Iceland is the navel of the world. If you doubt the veracity of this claim you need only consult the

Viking Sagas, the greatest of all literary achievements, where this view is expressed countless times during the course of long meandering tales of murder and revenge.

They point out that they have the biggest and best of many things. They have Vatnajökull, the largest glacier in Europe, with an area almost as large as Cyprus, which makes France's Mer de Glace look like an ice cube by comparison. Their waterfalls are higher, more powerful and more beautiful than any others in Europe. And even if Strokkur, their only surviving geyser, is smaller than the one in America's Yellowstone National Park, they are able to remind you that it can be found at Geysir, the Icelandic name now used to describe all such natural gushing phenomena. They also have the most westerly point in Europe, a place guaranteed to annoy the Irish who have erected numerous signs in Dingle claiming the same thing. Even the Icelandic pony gets in on the act, having five gaits rather than the four favoured by the rest of the world's horses.

> **Even the Icelandic pony gets in on the act, having five gaits rather than the four favoured by the rest of the world's horses.**

Icelanders see themselves as cultured and sophisticated, with an enviable literary heritage and independence of spirit. These points are always included in speeches by their presidents, who are seen as the embodiment of the nation and whose comments are quoted as gospel and prefaced with a friendly "As the president says…". In fact, so often is this phrase used that it has become a kind of valediction.


## How they see others

It might be imagined that the Icelanders, sharing a mutual heritage with the Scandinavian nations, would see them as brothers. Not so. Their isolation has meant that they still speak the language of the Vikings while the rest of the Scandinavians speak an inferior tongue comprising low German and a mishmash of other bits and pieces.

The Norwegians are laughed at for their enthusiasm for outdoor pursuits which is looked on as proof of what the Icelanders thought anyway, that the Norwegians are slow-witted and dull.

> **66 Their isolation has meant that they still speak the language of the Vikings while the rest of the Scandinavians speak an inferior tongue. 99**

Ask the Icelanders about the paintings of Munch, the music of Grieg and the books of Hamsun and they will tell you it is likely these individuals were descended from Icelandic Vikings who went home for the weekend and were stranded by a recalcitrant tide or wind. The discovery of North Sea oil and the fact that it has made the Norwegians very rich has led to a change of view. Now the

Norwegians are seen as slow-witted, dull, and quite disgustingly lucky.

The Swedes are considered to be self-centred, sex-mad and too frequently given to bouts of pleasure seeking – indulgences rather too close to their own not to resent them for it.

> **" The Swedes are considered to be self-centred, sex-mad and too frequently given to bouts of pleasure seeking. "**

Norwegians and Swedes are also disapproved of for being Arctic nations. With its name and its wild landscape Iceland might be expected to lie within the Arctic Circle, but only the island of Grimsey off the northern coast manages to do so, and then only by a few yards. As a consequence, Icelanders deride the Circle and say that only one man in Iceland can be bothered to cross it. He is the vicar of Grimsey and he only does so because the Circle runs through the centre of his bed.

The English are looked on as laughable and lovable eccentrics, much given to coming second. The Icelanders find this latter characteristic hilarious and strangely reassuring. Almost the whole population speaks English due to the one-time presence of an American air-force base in Iceland which meant that the nation was flooded with American television programmes. Local stations have replaced the direct American broadcasts, but as they mostly show American programmes it is difficult to notice a difference.

While the upstart Columbus gets the kudos for discovering the New World, the Icelanders revel in the knowledge that it was one of their own, Leifur Eríksson, who did so several centuries before. Some now wish he hadn't: as Churchill is reputed to have said, 'The Icelanders had the good sense to forget they had discovered America'. Icelanders like American dollars, but rather resented the servicemen who

> **66** The older generation have a saying: 'Danes make good rulers for Danes'. **99**

spent them. To get their own back, they banished the Americans to an inhospitable, lonely corner of the island on the pretext that Iceland's only international airport (Keflavík) is there. Oddly, if you ask, they will claim that Keflavík lies in this wilderness because it was built close to where the Americans were.

## Special relationships

The Icelanders have a special relationship with the Danes but this has nothing to do with their common Viking origin. Until the early 20th century Denmark ruled Iceland which is why the Icelanders see the Danes as having exploited their country, keeping it poor and uneducated, primitive and isolated. The older generation have a saying: 'Danes make good rulers for Danes', which is a roundabout way of saying that they should stay at home with their LEGO (though exceptions are made for Danes who are internationally famous, about whom older Icelanders can feel proprietorial).

Younger Icelanders are inclined to a different view of history. Danish is still taught in Icelandic schools (it was only replaced in 1998 by English as the primary foreign language), so youngsters develop an affinity with the Danes. They see them as cousins and can be wildly enthusiastic about them – as long as there are no Danes present.

**❝Luxembourg has the largest community of Icelandic ex-patriots in Europe.❞**

The only other nations with whom the Icelanders have any rapport are Luxembourgers, Canadians and Russians. Luxembourg has the largest community of Icelandic ex-patriots in Europe because the European headquarters of Icelandair used to be situated there. Icelanders share with the Luxembourgers an inferiority complex born of being so few in number. The Icelanders and the Luxembourgers do not often score high points in the Eurovision Song Contest* and regularly lose at football (though individual Icelanders are making an impact in European leagues).

The Canadian connection is a family one. As many as 10,000 Icelanders emigrated to Canada in the

---

* For this they are quite grateful. The Icelandic economy could not survive winning and having to stage the next event.

1880s, and ties have been maintained. When an Icelander meets a Canadian, the Canadian is expected to know the Canadian relatives of the Icelander he is speaking to.

The Russians are special for different reasons. Russian trawlers used to dock regularly and disgorge men of seemingly overwhelming stupidity who could be persuaded to

> **66 When an Icelander meets a Canadian, the Canadian is expected to know the Canadian relatives of the Icelander he is speaking to. 99**

exchange much-prized bottles of fierce vodka for clapped-out Ladas and other vehicles. Those who tasted the vodka had no doubt about who had the better deal. The Russians come less often now, but the love of fierce vodka remains.

## How they would like others to see them

They wish to be seen as they see themselves, as a highly cultured race. As proof of their sophistication, Icelanders are able to point to the publication of a monthly English-language newspaper. How many other countries produce a paper in a language other than their own?

It is equally impressive that, in this land of freezing temperatures, among the many traditional Icelandic maxims there is one that states: 'It is better to go barefoot than without books.'

# Character

## Strength and intelligence

The Vikings who settled Iceland in 870 were folk who could not tolerate the order imposed on their Scandinavian homelands by the king who had unified the countries. That independent disposition is still an Icelandic characteristic: the Icelander is an individualist and an adventurer.

The country also imposed itself on the national character. Those early settlers had a hard time. Then the climate eased and by the mid 12th century there was spare time to devote to fighting. Three groups of islanders fought on and off for nearly a century, a time now known as the 'Age of Sturlungar' from Sturla, a farmer from north of Reykjavík who was the father of Snorri Sturluson, one of Iceland's greatest poets, the author of *Egil's saga*. (It is said that Snorri maintained a herd of 120 cattle solely to produce the calves on whose skins he wrote his stories.)

> 66 Early settlers had a hard time. Then the climate eased and by the mid 12th century there was spare time to devote to fighting. 99

After the Age of Sturlungar the climate worsened which made fighting impossible: everyone's energy was consumed by staying alive. But the harsh, dark winters meant that the farmers had little to do but read and relate the sagas. This created a literate, artistically-minded people.

Their history gives rise to the dual personality of the Icelander. He values both his artistic heritage and his hardiness. The nation has survived appalling natural catastrophes; in 1783-5 the largest volcanic eruption the world has ever seen occurred killing a quarter of the population when the 'Haze of Hunger' (dust from the eruption) blocked out the sun. But the inhabitants shrugged it off. Today's Icelander draws comfort from this. He wants an Icelandic man to be the world's strongest, yet also wishes to be seen as a highly cultured person divorced from menial daily tasks.

> **66 Their history gives rise to the dual personality of the Icelander. He values both his artistic heritage and his hardiness. 99**

When Jón Páll Sigmarsson won the title of the world's strongest man he delighted all Icelanders during one part of the competition when he was required to lift a vast and improbable load above his head. As he raised it he said *"Ekkert mál fyrir Jón Pál"*. This translates as "No problem for John Paul", but in Icelandic it rhymes. The Icelanders were euphoric – Jón Páll had reinforced the national idea that the Icelander is a strong poet.

Not only has an Icelander held the title of World's Strongest Man, but there have been several Icelandic Miss Worlds. There have also been a surprising number of Icelandic chess grandmasters, and the nation has more writers and artists per capita than any other country on earth. These facts reinforce the Icelanders' belief that they are a nation of strong, beautiful and intelligent people.

## Self-sufficient and social

The Icelandic male may be individualistic, but he is also an 'associated man', addicted to clubs and groups. Most go to one or two gatherings each week – such as those of the Club for Humorous Pranks, or the Club for Wine Tasters Provided That Inebriation Does Not Lead to Divorce. Their enthusiasm for clubs does not extend as far as the joining of trades unions. They find such organizations altogether too earnest.

**❝ The Icelander is upset when his own achievements, however modest, are not greeted as earth shattering. ❞**

The life of the solitary farmer or fisherman may have made the Icelander appear withdrawn and silent, even shy, but this is now changing, travel having broadened him into a more sociable individual.

The Icelander is a hard worker, but erratic. He is self-reliant, flexible and long-suffering, but self-conscious, immodest and impatient. He is generous with regard to his friends, but also self-centred. He has little enthusiasm for the achievements of others, no matter how tremendous, but is upset when his own achievements, however modest, are not greeted as earth shattering.

Icelandic women are strong-willed and self-sufficient, both qualities dating from the fishing tradition, when the women organised the home and farm and managed everything while waiting for their men to return; often the men did not. Fishing communities have always had a high number of single mothers because of the shorter life expectancy of fathers. (There is still no social stigma attached to being a lone mother, married or otherwise. In fact, there are more single mothers than ever today and, along with Britain, Iceland has the highest illegitimate birthrate in Europe.)

Since they've maintained their strength and independence, feminism is seen as a backward step, for why accept equality when you have superiority? It is somewhat surprising that the modern Icelandic woman marries the modern Icelandic man. The only battleground of the sexes is politics where strong-minded women feel they have suffered at the hands of weak-minded men for years.

**66 Feminism is seen as a backward step, for why accept equality when you have superiority? 99**

## The farmer's mentality

Iceland came very quickly into the 20th century. Having been an isolated, insular race until 1940, the

Icelanders suddenly found themselves the centre of attention. Invaded (for their own good, or so they were told) by the British and Americans, they discovered that they were rich beyond their wildest dreams. New markets for their fish made them for many years the wealthiest nation in Europe. This happened to a simple country people, and rustic attitudes remained. It is said that in 1946 the Icelanders had the highest number of bath tubs per capita of any European country, but that more often than not their main use was for keeping fish fresh.

**66 The average farmer is considered well able to solve most of life's problems given 20 minutes, a hammer and a piece of string. 99**

The average farmer is considered well able to solve most of life's problems given 20 minutes, a hammer and a piece of string. This belief was reinforced by the country's early road builders who were book-trained engineers and proved to be quite useless. Even when they got it right, the bridges they built to connect outlying parts of the country to the main roads became an object of scorn: once the folk they were built to serve had used them to migrate to the towns, the bridges fell into disrepair and disuse behind them.

Being new to the concept of town-dwelling, the Icelanders still find its rules difficult. If you have been used to riding into the nearest village and hitching your horse to a rail outside the shop you want to visit, you expect to be able to do the same with your car. As a consequence, the underground car park in Reykjavík remained empty while the streets were full of cars whose drivers studiously ignored the parking meters. To combat this, the city authorities introduced an army of formidable parking wardens. So good have they been at their job that no-one now parks in the city centre at all and several shops in Laugavegur (the main street) have been forced to close down. There is now a (perhaps only tempo-rary) respite, the wardens having been dispatched to Laugardalur (Hot Spring Valley) where the new 'World Class' gym has attracted a clientele so unfit they are unable to walk the 200 metres from the car park and routinely park, illegally, outside the front entrance.

> **" If you are driving and see someone you know you will stop for a chat. The queue of vehicles behind the talkers will soon be miles long. "**

One custom has been maintained. If you are driving through town and see someone you know on the pave-ment or in a car coming the other way, you will stop for a chat, just as you would if you met him on horse-back. Such conversations last as long as they last. If that is a very long time, and it often is, the queue of vehicles behind the talkers will soon be miles long. The Icelanders tolerate this behaviour up to a point. Those who become sufficiently irate might blow their horns, but if they do this, the offending motorists and everyone else within earshot will fix them with a withering stare. However, there is an up-side. If someone is trying to cross a road, particularly when loaded with parcels, drivers will give way.

Rural attitudes have had odd repercussions. Icelanders made news some years ago by banning dogs from their towns. They told the world that the ban was due to problems with dog mess and the worms it carried. But the real reason was that the Reykjavík authorities thought dog-owning reeked too much of the rural past – the sophisticated town dweller didn't need a sheepdog. Dog owning is now allowed again though the cost of a dog licence is prohibitively expensive to reinforce official disapproval.

# Beliefs & Values

## The hold of the *Huldufólk*

Although it is not obvious to every visitor to the island, Iceland is inhabited by a whole host of folk besides the Icelanders. There are elves, who are about the size of ordinary people but mostly stay hidden from view. They live in hills. There are trolls. Unlike Norwegian trolls, the Icelandic troll is not small and ugly and does not live under a bridge in mortal fear of billy goats. Icelandic trolls are 10 to 12 feet tall and live in mountains. And there are dwarfs. Icelandic dwarfs are as tiny as might be expected and live in rocks. Collectively this army is known in Icelandic as *huldufólk* – hidden people, and their dwellings are easy to spot: they are exceptionally beautiful rocks, mountains and hills.

The visitor who thinks that all this is nonsense underestimates the hold the tales of hidden people have on the Icelandic mind. The landscape is so awesome that human beings cannot help

> **"Brought up on tales of a world peopled by curious gods and super-heroes, it is understandable that the Icelanders saw the land as the home of supernatural beings."**

but feel insignificant in relation to it. This was exacerbated by the early settlers living a life of solitude, well separated from their neighbours. (The farms had to be large as the soil was so poor.) Brought up on tales of the Viking past, of a world peopled with curious gods and superheroes, it is understandable that the Icelanders saw the land as the home of supernatural beings.

Belief runs so deep it is difficult to separate myth and reality. The main road from Reykjavík to Selfoss bears left for no apparent reason a few miles beyond Hveragerði, near a church on the right. It does this in order to avoid an elf hill. Even now, town streets are aligned to avoid elf hills and dwarf rocks. Past experience has taught the people that to attempt to build over a *huldufólk* site is useless. Bulldozers will fail, hammers will break, nothing can be done to destroy the site, so you might just as well go round it.

Today's youngsters are still told stories of the hidden people and enjoy the tradition because it adds something to their view of nature. But it is real enough to suggest that the old pagan Viking roots are closer to the surface than many Icelanders would care to admit.

A great grandmother will have told of the time her sheep went missing for a few days and an elf woman came to her door to apologise, saying she had needed ewe's milk for her sick infant, and telling her where the sheep could be found. At a public lecture about the *huldufólk*, when the speaker asked how many of the audience believed in elves, about 80% of those

**❝ When the speaker asked how many of the audience believed in elves, about 80% of those present raised their hands. ❞**

present raised their hands. Of them 50% had spoken to an elf and 25% had seen one. One Icelander living in Canada placed an advertisement in the national Icelandic newspaper for a female elf to go to Canada as companion to a male elf who had inadvertently travelled with a group of emigrating Icelanders. The male elf, starved of love and friendship, was making a nuisance of himself. The paper followed up the story hoping to join in the joke, but the advertiser wasn't joking, which probably didn't surprise the readers.

If you ask Icelanders about the hidden people you may well be told a story about Niels Bohr, the Danish physicist and Nobel prizewinner, with whom they feel a kinship since Iceland was under Danish rule when he was at the peak of his powers. At that time he had a lucky horseshoe

> **Having the last great wilderness in Europe, you would expect the Icelanders to be a green nation.**

hanging in his study. An incredulous visitor who found it hard to believe that so eminent a scientist could believe in such things, asked him outright. "Of course not," said Bohr, "but I'm told it works whether you believe it or not."

## Profit before protection

Having the last great wilderness in Europe, you would expect the Icelanders to be a green nation. This is not the case, at least not if green issues stand in the way of profit. But with the increasing importance of tourism to the economy there is a definite shift towards green. It is, after all, the colour of the American dollar.

The Icelanders have an ambivalent attitude towards nature. There are many National Parks set up to protect the best of the landscape, but a bounty is paid for shooting Arctic foxes, and there is an ongoing debate over the rights and wrongs of whaling. (The Icelandic expression for good luck is *hvelreki* which translates as 'May a whole whale wash up on your beach'.)

When the earliest settlers arrived in Iceland there were forests where now there are just mossy deserts. The trees were cut down for their longboats and soon there were no trees to speak of. There has been an attempt to create new woodland areas, but the climate means that trees grow slowly and are stunted by the wind. It is a national joke that if you are lost in an Icelandic forest all you need do is stand up. Curiously for a country which has so few trees, the Icelanders once erected the largest wooden cathedral in the whole of Scandinavia (using wood imported from Norway), and they still use wooden scaffolding which is attached to buildings by bits of string and electrical flex. Wood is easier on the hands when winter temperatures plummet. The lack of forests is ironic because one of the ways in which American soldiers, for whom Iceland was an unpopular posting, were encouraged to come to the island was to be told that there was a beautiful, blonde virgin beneath every tree.

> **It is a national joke that if you are lost in an Icelandic forest all you need do is stand up.**

## Family trees and fortunes

The ancient kings of Iceland being Danish, there is no Icelandic aristocracy. In its absence, and since the

Icelanders have realised that there are no classless societies in Europe, several 'classes' are developing.

One of the more interesting used to be a class based on family history. Since few families could trace their family back more than a few generations, those that could were proud of being able to point out that their ancestors had been the occupants of the first longboats to be drawn up on the southern beaches. But a vast database using information from the Sagas, church registers and census returns has allowed everyone to do the same. The result is that almost every Icelander now knows he is related to his next-door neighbour in some way. As a consequence the word 'uncle' is now used as a term of mutual description, for if you go back far enough it is probably true.

> **Almost every Icelander now knows he is related to his next-door neighbour in some way.**

Another class is education-based, and 'ill-educated' is an increasingly derogatory term. This is odd because the Icelanders have an abiding suspicion of education. Useful subjects in particular, such as science, engineering and languages, are not deemed to be worth studying. On the other hand, they are impressed by lawyers and doctors, and are also very fond of philosophers. A poor philosopher stands higher on the social scale than a technician or a good plumber, with the result that on occasions neither Icelandic theories nor Icelandic pipes hold water.

The most significant class is based on money. In this the Icelanders are no different from other nations, though enthusiasm for believing that the rich are a better class is taken to extremes. The rich must be better – they have a house abroad and a big car.

The Icelander is impressed by others' financial fortune, but envious of it. Any show of wealth is met by a public sneer – implying a dislike of ostentation – but a private grinding of teeth. In Iceland it is best to make your money quickly, before anyone knows what you're doing. Money, or the lack of it in comparison to others, causes great stress, and it is remarkable that life expectancy is still rising, rather than falling like a stone.

> **In Iceland it is best to make your money quickly, before anyone knows what you're doing.**

The Icelander's attitude to social standing is played out in the following scene. Early one morning some fishermen were making their way down to the shore for a day's fishing. They passed a house and as they did so the door opened and out came a group of professional men. A lawyer and a doctor, both unsteady on their feet, were carrying the paralytic form of the local mayor while a clergyman carried the mayor's hat. Seeing the fishermen, the group looked away, not because they were ashamed of themselves, but because in Icelandic society professionals are of superior standing and would not be caught dead conversing with rough fishing types. This neatly illustrates the Icelandic view that those at the top of the social pile, while enviably rich, are either daft or drunkards.

## Faith in fate

Like most nationalities the Icelanders are very religious in a crisis. Otherwise they are one of the least religious societies in Europe. The fatalism that was bred of fishing and a harsh climate led them in the past to attribute sufferings to God's will. Today God has been removed from the equation, but similar reasoning allows the Icelander to assume that everyone's problems are their own fault. Except for his own, of course.

# Obsessions

Politics and, in particular, the failings of politicians are a national obsession. But the chief obsession is:

## The weather

Icelanders are fond of saying that Iceland does not get real weather, just samples. They also say that if you don't like the weather you just have to wait five minutes and it will alter. What they really mean is that since the island is sandwiched between cold Arctic air heading south, and warm Gulf Stream air flowing north, it is prone to rapid change. It is possible to experience all four seasons in one day – the speed of the change depending on the strength of the wind.

**66 Iceland is close enough to the Arctic Circle to experience several weeks in December and January when it does not get light at all. 99**

Since the wind usually blows hard, a day that starts out badly, with rain and thick cloud, may be fine by midday. The Icelanders want the visitor to take heart from this. The problem is that if the weather is nice, all you have to do is wait five minutes and then it isn't.

Iceland is close enough to the Arctic Circle to see the midnight sun for several weeks in June and July. It is also close enough to experience several weeks in December and January when it does not get light at all. Winters are therefore rather more endured than enjoyed. People like the first snow because it heralds a white Christmas, but by February are sick of it and by April heartily sick of it. Spring never seems to come, and by the time it has finally arrived, autumn seems to be just around the corner.

Town dwellers mistreat the snow. It is ploughed, gritted, and generally abused until it ends up in dirty, sullen heaps at street corners, and on the islands in the middle of the road where it gobbles up the boots of the unwary, making crossing a road as hazardous as any expedition to the Pole. Just when the snow seems beaten, the daytime temperature rises and the heaps melt. But at nightfall it drops again and the whole wet mess freezes so that morning brings a pantomime of slipping people and sliding cars. Sometimes this sequence is repeated for a week or more, by the end of which everyone is short tempered and near suicidal.

## Trends and hi tech

The Icelanders have style. They suffer a climate that is best described as miserable but they don't allow it to get in the way of wearing the trendiest garb. If this decrees open-toed sandals, then that is what they will wear, even if the snow is four feet deep.

Style is learned early. Stand outside any school and you will be treated to a show of the latest in world fashion. A survey of teenagers in Reykjavík – aimed at proving

> **66** Style is learned early. Stand outside any school and you will be treated to a show of the latest in world fashion. **99**

that Iceland has the highest usage of mobile phones in Europe – failed to find a single 16-year-old girl who didn't have one.

People aspire to all the newest gadgets and gizmos, though this has as much to do with an obsession with technology and keeping up with the Magnussons as it has with style. If a new television model comes on the market it has to be purchased (and the old one can be put in the bedroom or kitchen). This overt materialism means that most Icelanders would almost prefer to live in a cardboard box than do without the latest hi-fi or electronic aid. But the box would be furnished and equipped to the highest standards.

Obsession with new technology means that the interior of the Icelandic house is state of the art but, in contrast, the electrics and plumbing of most houses are a mess. Even the best-appointed homes will have a light fitting hanging off the ceiling, and a leaking tap.

**66 Plants die quickly unless they are lovingly cared for, in which case they die slowly. 99**

The Icelanders' enthusiasm for interiors is not translated to the exterior. The climate is harsh. Plants die quickly unless they are lovingly cared for, in which case they die slowly. Gardening has not caught on, which means that the only fad not to have been imported from Europe or America is the garden centre. The climate also destroys any attempt to keep the outside of buildings tidy, so that even the smartest hotels have concrete external walls, the concrete blotched like an abstract painting. Buildings are roofed with corrugated iron which is regularly painted to keep it rust and leak free. Bright colours are cheaper than pastel ones, so the cheapest and brightest are used. The visually vibrant towns and villages appear to have been built by primary school children.

The obsession with the modern is in part a rejection of the Icelandic past and not everyone sees this as altogether a good thing. During a storm on the east coast, when high winds picked up a number of barbecues and deposited them out to sea, one commentator was moved to alter a well-known saying for bad weather – '*Það rignir eldi og eimyrju*' (It's raining fire and iron) – a saga reference to the heat of battle – to announce that it was raining fire and grills, a sardonic view of the 'suburbanisation' of the nation.

Style is expensive, but since it is essential to their way of life, Icelanders live on credit cards and borrowed money. Next to their cars and electronic gadgetry, their credit rating is the closest thing to the Icelanders' heart. Credit cards are accepted in all hotels and shops, down to the smallest kiosk. Indeed, if you just want a tube of toothpaste and offer a shop assistant cash, it will be assumed that you have no credit rating at all.

**❝ If you just want a tube of toothpaste and offer a shop assistant cash, it will be assumed that you have no credit rating at all. ❞**

You will be pointed out to other assistants and followed around. After all, if you have been reduced to using cash it is possible that you are a shoplifter.

These days things are not that straightforward. Large, expensive four-wheel drive cars sport notices saying that the owner is willing to give it to anyone

willing to take over the credit payments. However
Icelanders are optimistic. Surviving natural disasters is
part of life, so the global glitch is seen as just an
unfortunate enforced rest until the next credit boom.

# Behaviour

The typical Icelander is quiet and restrained in the
company of strangers. In any meeting he is the man
who says nothing and is amazed by those who ask
questions. Special amazement is reserved for people
who, like the Americans, are able to talk for an hour
on a particular subject – two if they actually know
anything about it. By contrast, the
Icelander will have difficulty in
filling five minutes, even if he is a
world authority.

> **66 In any meeting the typical Icelander is the man who says nothing and is amazed by those who ask questions. 99**

To encounter the typical
Icelander, go to the Prikið café in
Reykjavík. Here the men of
Iceland come early, long before any of the shops have
opened, to drink coffee. They sit in gloomy silence,
their noses thrust deep into newspapers. Should anyone utter a sound he will receive the censorious stares
usually reserved for those who sneeze in a library. In
one corner sits an old man with a deerstalker hat and
a stiff moustache. He reads *Morgunblaðið*, the nation-

al daily, and sips coffee with an air of suspicion. Sit there all day and you will never see him leave. But if you should take your eyes off him for a moment, when you look again you will notice that he has been replaced by another, almost identical, man.

Public restraint is not matched by private diffidence. On a one-to-one basis the Icelander is talkative, the high esteem in which he holds himself breaking through the shyness. He will assume you wish to know his opinion about anything and everything. The fact that what he has to say may well be irrelevant to your circumstances, or the matter in hand, will be of little

> **On a one-to-one basis the Icelander is talkative, the high esteem in which he holds himself breaking through the shyness.**

importance to him. He is an Icelander, you are an audience (however small), so you will be told. In the main his opinions will be worthwhile and interesting, but if they are not you will be in for a sorry time, for when the Icelander is boring he is very boring indeed.

## Family bonds

The Icelanders have a strong sense of family. Children help with the chores and despite increased affluence and satellite television there is a marked absence of the teenage conflict that affects other European nations. Perhaps this is because family life is less frantic. School hours are less lengthy than in the rest of Europe so there is more time for their social lives. Alternatively it could be that another old farming tradition lives on – that, as long as the children behave marginally better than the sheep, they will be left in peace.

However, with more and more mothers having (or choosing) to go out to work, children – never over-supervised or disciplined – are now free to roam at will, occasionally to the aggravation of others. One of the joys of Icelandic society is that, despite the annoyance this may cause, there is no fear that the kids will be harmed by anyone. Icelanders view societies in which children cannot play outside for fear of being molested as very sick indeed.

**66 As long as the children behave marginally better than the sheep they will be left in peace. 99**

There is, though, one tradition which brings the Icelanders into conflict with the rest of Europe. In Iceland mothers have placed their infants, from the age of three months, on balconies outside the family apartment for an afternoon nap, even in the depths of winter. The fresh, cold air was deemed good for them, and so it has proved given the general health of the nation. But when an Icelandic mother carried on the tradition in Germany, neighbours reported her to the police for cruelty. The same thing has happened in Sweden. Icelanders are perplexed: surely there are worse things to do to a child than improve its welfare?

Although the trend is now for the old folk to go into purpose built homes, it used to be quite usual for parents to move in with their children when old age made life difficult for them. It was not uncommon for a father to turn up on the doorstep of his daughter a day or two after the funeral of the mother. "Well," he would say, "here I am, where do you want me to sleep?"

## No hex on sex

It is claimed that wherever foreign trawlers docked in Iceland many years ago there are now quite a few dark-haired, dark-eyed children. One place in the eastern fjords was even euphemistically called Congo as a result. This suggests that the Icelandic attitude to sex was always fairly liberal, sex being seen as a fun activity to be indulged in often, rather than something that was done with the lights off. Things haven't changed.

> **Liberal attitudes mean that the Icelandic man has never bothered to develop a series of 'chat up' lines.**

Liberal attitudes mean that the Icelandic man has never bothered to develop a series of 'chat up' lines. A straightforward 'yes' or 'no' is all the conversation which occurs before the action starts. Whereas in most of the rest of Europe an invitation to 'come in for a coffee' is seen as a step on a road that might (but might not) lead to bed, in Iceland the coffee is served after, as a present for services rendered. As a result, Icelandic women like foreign males who spend half the night 'chatting them up' before moving on to the main event.

When Iceland appointed Jóhanna Sigurðardóttir as interim Prime Minister the world's media were not at all interested in her politics, only the fact that she was openly lesbian, the first such leader in the modern world. To Icelanders this was the least interesting fact about her. Iceland decriminalized gay sex as long ago as 1940. For them the point of interest was that for the first time in their history the government had an equal number of men and women.

**66 The local attitude to things sexual is epitomised by the Icelandic Museum of Phallology which has a display of 80 penises from over 30 species of mammal. 99**

The local attitude to things sexual is epitomised by the Icelandic Museum of Phallology which has a display of 80 penises from over 30 species of mammal, together with a collection of related oddments. Though the museum does not yet have a human specimen on show, the proprietor has been given the promise of one by a farmer who is over 80 – but only when it is no longer in regular use.

## On time is any time

With instincts adapted from time immemorial to the whims of wind and sea, Icelanders are notoriously unpunctual. Their partners in the European Economic Area have come to regard this as a joke, for if a meeting was planned for 9 a.m., the Germans would arrive at 9 a.m. precisely and the Dutch at 8.40 a.m., but the Icelanders would turn up when they felt like it.

## Shove while you shop

On Saturday mornings there is a market in Reykjavík's customs house. Stalls sell everything from motor bike bits to washing machines and the latest PCs. Junk and secondhand CDs are the most popular items. Icelanders flock to it, not just for the bargains on offer but for the opportunity it gives them to ignore queues and to barge and shout. It also allows them to finger the goods on offer, something to which they are strangely addicted.

> **With instincts adapted from time immemorial to the whims of wind and sea, Icelanders are notoriously unpunctual.**

Shops open at 10 a.m. Visitors who arrive in Iceland on a Friday assume this is because Friday night lasts until Saturday morning when the last of the revellers has gone home. In fact, the shops open at 10 a.m. every day to give those who are not working a leisurely start to the day.

A first-time visitor to Iceland could be forgiven for

believing that every shop assistant in the land is called Hilda, for that, apparently, is what every Icelander calls out when he is in a shop. In fact, he is shouting "*Heyrðu*" which means "here", or "me next". Icelanders are the friendliest, most caring people you

> **66 The Icelanders do not feel themselves bound by the conventions of polite society. 99**

could hope to meet. But in a busy shop, don't get between an Icelander and the shop counter. He will ignore signs pleading for tolerance in public places in favour of the elbow. Shopping involves selecting your item and then pushing and shoving your way to the front of the throng at the counter, all the while shouting "*Heyrðu*". To an Icelander the idea of queuing, let alone the queue itself, is anathema, and he is seen at his worst in the state alcohol shops, especially on a Friday night. In supermarkets he will wait in sullen line for his turn at the till, but only because the check-out areas have been constructed to be one person wide.

# Manners

## Meeting and greeting

The Icelanders do not feel themselves bound by the conventions of polite society. They do not go in for formalities such as 'Good morning. How are you?'

Their towns are little more than villages and, as with all villages, most of the inhabitants know each other – either as ex-schoolmates, workmates, or – as shown by the national database – 'uncles'. A quiet morning's shopping can turn into an epic journey through your past life. Just stopping to say hello can turn a quick trip into one requiring three days' leave from work.

To control time loss, many Icelanders dispense with the usual conventions, but for those who do not put their heads down and ignore everyone they pass, elaborate rules of engagement exist. Ex-schoolmates who have not been seen for several years are not acknowledged unless they were particular friends who have moved from the area; a wave suffices for ex-workmates; and for those seen frequently, the standard handshake is used. For distant relatives a handshake – friendly but not too warm – and an enquiry about an old aunt are enough, though a hug might be required if they are rich. A hug and a coffee is much better if they are both rich and old.

> **" A quiet morning's shopping can turn into an epic journey through your past life. "**

The Icelanders used to be a more tactile race, the kissing of friends and relatives being the norm, but this gradually came to be seen as altogether too familiar and was stopped. However, the French habit of almost kissing both cheeks is becoming fashionable and has re-awakened their enthusiasm for touching.

# Leisure & Pleasure

The most pleasurable thing the Icelanders can do is spend money, especially if they haven't got any. Gambling, however, does not much appeal to them. This is fortunate because, apart from the state lottery, gambling is only permitted by a charitable organisation or the University. However, there are many other things to spend money on.

## Seeking the sun

Given the fact that in Iceland bathing in the sea brings on hypothermia in seconds and sunbathing is likely to produce acres of gooseflesh long before it produces a tan, Icelanders dream of holidays in Spain and Florida. Foreign travel was difficult for so long that the novelty of going abroad has not worn off.

## A hut above the rest

All town-dwelling Icelanders have timber-built huts out in the middle of nowhere a couple of hours' drive from town. Their idea is to use them during spring and summer to escape the rigours of urban living, to rediscover their Icelandic roots, and to be at one with nature. However, as the town-dwelling Icelander lives in town precisely to avoid the rigours of the country that so plagued his grandfather and father, the huts are rarely

36

visited. They are maintained solely to impress the neighbours.

## Winter sport

It is a myth that the Icelander is a hearty outdoor type who finds his country a rugged arena for pursuits which require large boots and a beard. When the snow scooter and glacier-driving fans have departed for home, the hardy few that are left are foreign skiers. Most

> 66 The newer the sport the better they like it, and if it requires a large amount of expensive equipment, they like it even more. 99

Icelanders stay indoors during the winter, peering out anxiously every morning to see if spring has arrived. Or else do the sensible thing and go to Spain.

## Summer sport

The Icelanders will try their hand at anything. The newer the sport the better they like it, and if it requires a large amount of expensive equipment, they like it even more. Sport for children is well organised, and individuals do well. Several Icelanders play pro-fessional football in Germany, Scandinavia and Britain. In team games Iceland does about as well on the world stage as any medium-sized town would expect to do, though they do excel at handball.

The national sport is *glíma*, a form of wrestling.

*Glíma* is unique to Iceland, though it has similarities to the wrestling practised in Western Samoa. No clear link has been established, and it does seem a long way to go for practice. The sport is very old and involves the wearing of traditional belts and much prancing about before the action starts.

> **66 Golf is currently the fastest growing sport in the country. In summer the game can be, and is, played all night as well as all day. 99**

Golf is currently the fastest growing sport in the country with over 50 golf courses and clubs. Iceland's position is a help to those who are unable to book a game. In summer the game can be, and is, played all night as well as all day.

## Car crazy

People are always on the move, dropping the children off, going shopping, picking the children up again, going swimming. Reykjavík appears to have twice the number of vehicles that a city its size would normally have because Icelanders do everything by car.

But they also drive to such an extent that driving can be considered a leisure activity. Young Icelanders mix this dubious pleasure with that of drinking Coca-Cola, one hand on the steering wheel, the other holding aloft a can or bottle. They drive round the towns endlessly, a practice which has become so common it has been given a name – the *rúntur*, literally the round tour. When the *rúntur* became passé in Reykjavík, it moved on to Akureyri. This town being further north, the custom is for the occupants of the car, usually male, to wear clothes suitable for Californian beaches, turning the car's heater up full to compensate for the Icelandic temperature.

> 66 The custom is for the occupants of the car to wear clothes suitable for Californian beaches. 99

Icelanders drive all winter long, for in spite of its name only 11% of Iceland is covered by permanent glaciers, and the winters are harsh only in the remote centre of the country. No-one could live in the hostile interior, a place so lunar-like that N.A.S.A. took its astronauts there to train for landing on the moon.

Everyone lives on the coast, where the temperature rarely stays below freezing for very long periods, and snowfalls, although regular, are more of a nuisance than a hazard. Most drivers carry a spade in the boot as a precaution, and if they don't have a four-wheel drive vehicle, studded tyres, though not compulsory, are absolutely essential.

Four-wheel drive vehicles being a modern invention, all Icelanders must have one, so the roads are frequented by these huge machines, custom-fitted with massive wheels which threaten to drive over the top of any ordinary car daft enough to get in the way – like something straight out of *Terminator 2*.

In summer, Icelanders drive their RVs (motorhomes) all over the country for the satisfaction of being able to park them on some lonely spot for no particular reason. Other road users are driven to distraction as the cumbersome beasts take up all the road and drive very slowly. In winter the inhabitants will often be seen dragging horseboxes or vast trailers. These are for snow scooters, which a number of people delight in hauling out of town to (perhaps the same) lonely spots, unloading with great effort, and then driving aimlessly for an hour or so – just for the thrill of making tracks in the snow.

> **Icelanders drive their RVs all over the country for the satisfaction of being able to park them on some lonely spot for no particular reason.**

For some, even this thrill is inadequate, and there are those who fit even bigger wheels and tyres and drive off-road (although in view of the state of the roads this is something of a moot point), tackling snowfields, mountains and glaciers. This form of entertainment was invented by an Icelander, which is just as likely to be due to the fact that no other country could come up with anyone crazy enough to do so as it is to the quality of the northern intellect. Icelanders drive to places most people would not want to visit.

Infatuation with hi tech does not end with the vehicle itself. It will be kitted out with a telephone and e-mail, a television and a CB radio. There is also likely to be a satellite navigation set. This is particularly handy if the vehicle happens to disappear into a glacial crevasse. The set, being accurate to just a few metres, will be able to tell the occupants almost precisely where they died.

## Movies and popcorn

Measured against the population there are four times as many cinemas in a big Icelandic town as there are in other countries. The Icelanders like the cinema, but not just for the films, which are mainly American or English and have sub-titles rather than being dubbed. Most of the audience follow the dialogue, but use the sub-titles to help out, which means they do not have to catch every spoken word. This is an advantage because the other reason for going to the cinema

66 There is also likely to be a satellite navigation set. This is particularly handy if the vehicle happens to disappear into a glacial crevasse. 99

is to consume vast quantities of popcorn and to drink huge vats of Coca-Cola. As soon as the film starts, so does the noise, created by hundreds of munching jaws and the crackling of corn, followed by the slurping of hundreds of straws.

After about 45 minutes, right in the middle of a critical scene, the film stops and the lights go up. The consequence of the drinking is now apparent: the audience rises as one and flocks out. Ten minutes later everyone reappears, re-supplied with large containers, and the whole procedure starts again.

## Partying the night away

The Icelanders are great ones for entertainment. Centuries of making their own amusement in turf huts during the long dark winters have left them in permanent need of company. As a result there is a huge number of things to do and places to go in the towns – theatres, clubs for all kinds of music, discos, restaurants.

**66 The weekend starts at midnight, none of the clubs closing before 6 a.m., when everybody moves on to a party. 99**

For the committed drinker the weekend starts on Friday afternoon at home. It starts there because it is cheaper to drink at home than in a bar. The rule, therefore, is to drink heavily at home, going out just to finish the job off in the company of a few like-minded people.

For the rest of the population the weekend starts at midnight, none of the clubs closing before 6 a.m., when everybody moves on to a party. Dancing was outlawed by the Danes who believed that the high level of illegitimate births in Iceland was attributable to it. After Home Rule had been established, the ban was lifted. The Icelanders, being a more intelligent people, had worked out that dancing was not the cause.

## Old time entertainment

A famous old Icelandic book of games for all the family includes one that involved lying people down on their backs, putting a coin on their nose, and laughing at the faces they pulled as they tried to flick the coin off without using their hands. Another game was a race between two groups of four people who passed eggs to one another using spoons held in the mouth. Again, no hands were allowed, and the eggs were real. No wonder Icelanders were grateful when television arrived.

## Ads for fads

American television was available at an early stage of broadcasting history in Iceland. The populace was appalled by the crassness of the advertisements, and since none of the advertised goods was actually for sale in Iceland, they were able to reinforce their cultural snobbery by noting frequently and at length that they were far too intelligent to be hoodwinked by such rubbish. However, when the single Icelandic TV channel offered advertising, one company used the saturation technique to sell a foot massager. It was allegedly both useless and unnecessary, but by the end of the campaign it is estimated that 50% of Icelandic houses had one and that no-one had used it more than once.

The audience is becoming more sophisticated and the most popular show is performed by a group of four middle-aged men who, each Saturday throughout the winter, re-enact scenes from Icelandic life which mix comedy with political satire. Other shows involving the Icelanders themselves are also popular: due to the small size of the population, almost every Icelander will appear on the show at some time. Why else would people watch?

> **66 Everybody has to invent and speak a four-line verse that humorously insults one or more of his fellow guests. 99**

# Conversation & Gestures

## The joy of the jibe

A famous Icelandic poet used four-line verses to insult his contemporaries. The short verses were humorous, but cutting. In doing this the poet was not creating something new, but reinforcing a tradition that was centuries old. Even today there are gatherings where everybody has to invent and speak a four-line verse that humorously insults one or more of his fellow guests.

44

The essence of Icelandic conversation is the insult. Icelanders are born with a talent for it and use it with ease from an early age. Because of their farming and fishing ancestry the most telling jibes involve sheep and fish. It is a very serious matter to refer to someone as a sheep or a codhead. (In fact the Icelander is more likely to be offended by a suggestion that he is a sheep than that his father had a marked preference for ewes over women.) Equally potent is the suggestion that the Icelander is *púkalegur*, literally a peasant. You will be implying that he is lazy, stupid or uncultured. All these might be true, though laziness is far from being a national characteristic, but that is beside the point.

In conversation, the Icelanders are wonderfully free of the English habit of meaning something other than what is actually said. Once a subject has been brought up for discussion, all aspects of it can be thoroughly and honestly explored – though this does not mean that all topics of conversation are allowed.

> **Because of their farming and fishing ancestry the most telling jibes involve sheep and fish. It is a very serious matter to refer to someone as a sheep or a codhead.**

Never ask how much an Icelander earns, and in no circumstances criticise his driving.

Despite the long tradition of swapping insults, there has never been an Icelandic tradition of gestures, rude or otherwise. So they import them. For instance, they have adopted the German one of tapping the side of the forehead to indicate stupidity. This is seen as genuinely offensive. If a driver intends making this sign to someone who has cut in on him while driving in town, he will first scan the road ahead to ensure there is no set of traffic lights in sight.

# Systems

## More rut than road

Iceland is big. It is a bit bigger than Ireland, almost three times the size of Belgium, and the same size as Kentucky. To drive around it takes days.

In part this is due to the fact that, because of the harsh climate, roads are at best poor and at worst dreadful. Those travelling to Þingvellir, site of the world's oldest parliament, will find the road good, being metalled all the way there and around the bend. Þingvellir is set in a raised circle of grass beside a volcanic rift, and is an almost compulsory item on the itinerary of every Icelandic tour company. The vast majority go no further than this, so do not know that beyond the next bend the road reverts to the Icelandic norm – a gravel track that frequently degenerates into a gravel

**66 Iceland is big. It is a bit bigger than Ireland, and the same size as Kentucky. To drive around it takes days. 99**

track interspersed with pot holes. A journey takes on epic proportions as you weave between the holes, desperately hoping for a length of road that will not interfere with your digestion.

Periodically a landslip, caused by summer rain, winter snow, or volcanic activity, will inundate the road. The Icelanders remain unfazed by this, merely calling out a steam roller to flatten the soil heap and then driving on the top. As a result in some places the road lies several feet above the surrounding land.

At intervals a curious sign – *blindhæð* – indicates that the next section should be driven with care as the road is about to go over a hump. Despite the fact that in this sparsely

> **66** Periodically a landslip, caused by summer rain, winter snow, or volcanic activity, will inundate the road. **99**

populated country it is possible to drive all day without actually getting anywhere or meeting anyone, the hump will always be concealing the one car that is coming in the opposite direction.

To help the poorly sighted at pedestrian crossings in Reykjavík, a ticking noise has been added to the green 'walk' signal. The noise is all but inaudible, but when someone does hear it, they usually assume that one of the hidden people has become trapped inside the device and is knocking to be let out. By the time the confusion is over, the 'walk' light has changed to red.

## Public transport

Iceland has excellent air services. Keflavík is probably the most beautiful international airport in the world and certainly the only one built on a piece of land obtained a thousand years ago in exchange for an embroidered cloak. For internal flights the airport close to Reykjavík is kept buzzing: the tedium of driving long distances makes flying the popular choice. Thus the skies above Iceland are patterned with airborne Icelanders speeding about, just as they do on the ground.

> **66 The skies above Iceland are patterned with airborne Icelanders speeding about, just as they do on the ground. 99**

The bus system is equally efficient. Given a few weeks one can travel all the way around the island, stopping off to see things and then hopping back on the bus again. It can pose a problem though, when on a Monday morning the reply to the question "When is the next bus?" is "Wednesday afternoon". Bus stops are not well equipped for those who decide to wait.

You can't catch a train because there aren't any.

## Powered by nature

In spite of having no coal or oil, Icelanders are blessed with lashings of natural hot water from geothermal origins which is used to make 90% of Iceland's electricity in a way that is pollution-free and cheap. This water is also used to provide central-heating systems in the houses; it is metered and paid for by the gallon. Even the waste water – which is still quite warm – is used, pipes being run under the pavements to melt the winter's snow and ice. The system is not organised by the town councils, so individual householders have to pay for the pipes to be installed. It is therefore possible to walk along a street that has a snow heap requiring mountaineering skills, then a section of clean, wet pavement, then a tricky iced section where pipes do not exist, and then another snow mountain. It pays to be alert.

Already one step ahead of the world with these methods, Iceland wants to phase out its dependency on oil by 2050. An experiment with hydrogen-powered vehicles is under way and a number of these in the form of hire cars and buses already exist. Hydrogen is produced with water and electricity (of which Iceland has an abundance) so this would greatly aid the economy as oil is extremely expensive to ship to Iceland. There is however a slight inconvenience: currently only one hydrogen filling station exists, which means a journey of only 160km before needing to fill up again. So you can safely assume that setting out for a Sunday spin is definitely out of the question.

> **66 Even the waste water is used, pipes being run under the pavements to melt the winter's snow and ice. 99**

## Distant degrees

State education (and health care) is so good that there is no need for private systems. Formal education starts when children are six, though there are plenty of pre-school groups that take children from three years old for the day or half-day. Compulsory schooling lasts from six to 16, after which there is high school until the age of 20.

At this stage many youngsters either go abroad or go on to university. There are two universities in Reykjavík, another in Akureyri plus two agricultural colleges, but Iceland does not have the resources to cover all subjects, so if you want to study subjects such as architecture or postgraduate medicine you must go abroad, and a staggering number of students do so.

**❝State education (and health care) is so good that there is no need for private systems.❞**

Overseas travel has advantages and disadvantages. On the one hand, returning students can see their homeland as small and parochial and find it wanting. On the other hand, returning students bring a cosmopolitan element to Iceland. Two students from America who have studied the same discipline together in Europe, might live 3,000 miles apart and never see or hear of each other again after they get home, but Icelanders in a similar situation may live in adjacent streets and meet up in the supermarket.

## Emergency services

There is a very efficient coastguard service which more or less stands in for army, navy and air force. During the Cod Wars a coastguard boat with an antique cannon mounted on the front was more than a match for the British Royal Navy.

As nothing seems to burn down during the Icelandic winter, the fire brigade spends its time making savings for the health service. This is done by having the firemen remove

> **66 In winter firemen remove icicles the size of the Sword of Damocles which hang menacingly from the gutterings of high buildings. 99**

icicles the size of the Sword of Damocles which hang menacingly from the gutterings of high buildings.

In the summer months the brigade deals with a few fires. It cannot fill in its time by rescuing the odd cat stuck in a tree. There are no trees for it to get stuck in.

## Law & Order

The police, who are known as *löggan*, a shortened form of the Icelandic for 'servant of the law', are liked. Little boys want to grow up to be policemen, though this may have something to do with their being unable to be train drivers.

The police are hot on speeding, and all cop cars are fitted with radar speed guns. They are even hotter on drink-driving. The merest suspicion of alcohol in a driver's blood and he is in very hot water indeed.

Most crime is drink-related, the Icelanders being aggressive when they have had too much to drink. Window breaking is popular, particularly with Iceland's glaziers, as a stroll downtown on a Sunday morning will demonstrate. Occasionally a drunken brawl results in a death and someone is charged with manslaughter. Murder is very unusual, so rare, in fact, that a murder in the north of the country in the early 19th century still attracts debate. When another took place in 1990, the *löggan* called in a detective from Hamburg because they felt so out of their depth. In the nature of finding a way of making cash from virtually any situation, the guilty party has written a best-selling book on salmon fishing.

> 66 Murder is very unusual, so rare, in fact, that a murder in the north of the country in the early 19th century still attracts debate. 99

The only serious white-collar crime is tax evasion which costs the state millions every year, but most Icelanders show little concern as the state is seen as fair game. If someone is caught it is felt to be more bad luck than justice, though an exception might be made for the directors of the country's three fuel import companies who met every month to carve up the market between them. They failed to notice, or misunderstood the significance, when policing was passed to the European Economic Area, and consequently faced trial under anti-competition laws.

# Sense of Humour

A man was driving in the wilds of Iceland when his car suddenly stopped. He was not much of a mechanic, but in desperation he lifted up the bonnet and peered at the engine. He was shaking his head in exasperation when a voice beside him said, "It's your carburettor." Turning, he found himself face to face with a horse. He fled in fright, running over the brow of a nearby hill. Below he saw a farm and hurtled down to it. He banged on the door and the farmer let him in. He poured out the story to the farmer who sat impassively. When he had finished the farmer said, "What colour was the horse?" The man, stunned by the question, replied "Brown". "Ah," said the farmer, "take no notice of him. That one knows nothing about cars."

> **Standard Icelandic humour is an acquired taste, one not normally shared by outsiders.**

Another man was hauling in the trawl on a fishing boat when the trawl pulled violently and a cord severed two of his fingers. Horrified, the man rushed to the bridge to show the captain. "Look," he said, holding up his hand to reveal the bleeding stumps, "I've lost two fingers." The captain eyed him for a moment and then said "Not in here".

These are unusual Icelandic jokes in that everybody can appreciate them. Standard Icelandic humour is an acquired taste, one not normally shared by outsiders.

53

For instance, the whole island rocked with laughter at the tale of an Icelandic woman who married a Turk. When the marriage failed, a long legal battle ensued which ended with the man taking their children off to Turkey. To get her revenge, the woman ate turkey for Christmas. (It can only be assumed that the joke is in the telling, or that the endless dark nights of winter do something to the brain cells.)

It has long been said that the Icelanders have no sense of humour at all. The grim-faced expression that is the norm (born of facing into the winter wind) rarely cracks into a smile. But they do have their own humour. It is derived from odd people and odd situations, with a special fondness for the surreal. As might be expected from a people with a long tradition of literacy, it also relies heavily on word play and spontaneity. In that sense it is akin to British humour, with puns and spoonerisms featuring strongly. A fine example of this is the description of two farms in the south of the country. For reasons lost in time one is called Grave. The other is called On the Edge of the Grave.

**66 Icelanders do have their own humour. It is derived from odd people and odd situations, with a special fondness for the surreal. 99**

Much of the humour is kindly. In the Westmann Islands, off the southern coast of Iceland, lived a man named Guðjón. During his twenties he moved to

Reykjavík on three separate occasions, each time failing to settle and returning home. From then on, until his death at the age of 81, he was affectionately known by his nickname, Guðjón *flækingur* (Guðjón the Wanderer).

Icelanders do have two groups of unfortunates whom they make the butt of acerbic humour. They tell jokes about the over-healthy Norwegians

> **" In Hafnarfjörður the inhabitants walk quietly past the pharmacies so as not to wake the sleeping pills. "**

and their passion for sport. But mostly they joke about the inhabitants of Hafnarfjörður, a town a few miles from Reykjavík.

In Hafnarfjörður the inhabitants walk quietly past the pharmacies so as not to wake the sleeping pills; the refuse carts do 100 m.p.h. in case they are robbed; the children take ladders when they start at high school, and their parents take the same ladders shopping if they hear that prices are higher this week. The Icelandic expression for when the pavements are slippery is that they are covered in 'flying ice'. If the weather forecast predicts flying ice, Hafnies (people from Hafnarfjörður) sit outside in the cold all night, their eyes glued to the heavens for fear of missing this strange spectacle. Hafnies are also known as *gaflarars* – from *gafl* (gable) – because they are said to lean under the eaves of their roofs all day waiting for the world to come around the corner for an idle gossip.

The tone of the humour is such that the Hafnies tell the jokes too and have even turned them to their advantage. A Friends of Hafnarfjörður Society has been formed to promote the tall stories (no ladder required) and so gain commercial advantage, and the best Hafnie jokes are now told by Hafnies themselves.

# Culture

## It's a continuing saga

The great Icelandic sagas were written in the 12th, 13th and early 14th centuries and have been nourishing Icelandic culture ever since. Many people ask in all seriousness whether there would have been an Iceland without the sagas, such a powerful peg are they on which to hang nationhood. The Icelanders are well pleased that it was their Viking ancestors who produced these works, there being no equivalent from Denmark, Norway or Sweden. It is, however, a myth that today's Icelander can read the original texts without transcription, so difficult is the Gothic script.

> **Great Icelandic sagas were written in the 12th, 13th and early 14th centuries and have been nourishing Icelandic culture ever since.**

As a result of constant re-evaluation, the sagas are as alive now as they were when they were written. Until recently every day on prime-time radio there was a 15-minute reading from one of the sagas followed by a 15-minute discussion on the issues the passage raises. It is thought likely to be revived any day, so popular was the programme. The sagas are of such importance to the national culture that they form the basis of many a modern tale. Among the best is that of a truculent taxi driver who was stopped by four students on their way to a celebratory evening. Aware that he was the only car for miles around, he decided to make sure that they were worthy of his services. He said he would only take them if they were able to quote accurately the first line of *Njál's saga*. One of the students could, so he happily transported them. It is difficult to think of another European country in which a taxi driver could set such a puzzle and a student be able to answer it.

> **66** More books are published in Iceland per head of population than in any other country, and they are of the highest quality. **99**

## Write on

More books are published in Iceland per head of population than in any other country, and they are of the highest quality. Although prices are outlandish, they sell in large quantities. So while it is said that if you offer a book to an Englishman for Christmas he will say 'No thanks, I've already got one', an Icelander will be thrilled at the prospect and spend the afternoon going through the shelves of all the local bookshops.

It is an Icelandic saying that if there is a topic in life then there must be a book on it. To make sure this is true, all Icelanders write, some of them profusely. Indeed, writing is a national pastime.

A major figure of the Icelandic literary scene is Nobel laureate Halldór Laxness. A passage from his work *Heimsljós* (World Light) shows why he deserves such recognition:

> 'Where the glacier reaches up to the sky, the land ceases to be of this world and becomes a part of heaven; there can be no more sorrows there and therefore joy is no longer necessary, beauty alone rules, beyond any claims.'

The favourite medium is poetry, sometimes in the scaldic metre, a rhythm unique to Iceland largely because no-one else cares enough to use it. One aspect of the scaldic poem is its use of metaphor, the more complicated, and therefore unintelligible, the better. Thus no *skáld* (the term used for a scaldic poet) would dream of calling the sky the sky, not when he could call it 'the hero's hall', or of calling men men, when they could be 'the food of wolves'. A favourite theme is the retelling of the great epics, full of lyrical passages about the beauty of the sun going down over the fish-drying frames on cold, misty days in autumn. It is rumoured that one day Reykjavík will be adorned by a new statue raised in memory of the lone Icelander who never wrote a poem.

## The art of the matter

The visual arts are close to the heart of all Icelanders. The country experiences over 20 earthquakes every day, and though most are minor, the landscape must never be taken for granted. This fluidity is reflected in Icelandic sculpture and painting. Many people sculpt or paint in their spare time. It is as though the creativity of the Icelandic landscape is reflected in the creativity of its people. There being little vegetation to cover the geology, Iceland, like the Pompidou Centre in Paris, wears its bones on the outside.

> 66 The country experiences over 20 earthquakes every day, and though most are minor, the landscape must never be taken for granted. 99

## An orchestral feat

There are fine Icelandic composers, such as Jón Leifs and Atli Heimir Sveinsson and, most popular of all, Sigvaldi Kaldaóns, an impecunious country doctor who spent his spare time composing. Their music is played by the National Orchestra. The fact that Iceland has a National Orchestra is remarkable, not only because so small a country can afford to maintain one, but because enough people can be found to form one.

## The music of ice

Choral singing is an Icelandic tradition. It is said that wherever you get three people together they will start singing in 4-part harmony.

In rock music, the success of Björk Guðmundsdóttir, the elfin-like pop singer, is not the country's only impact on the world of music. Sigur Rós, a group best described as post-rock, has a huge fan base. Their minimalist style is said to 'take tiny musical fragments and then go on vast journeys'. The upbeat songs echo the strivings of ancestral Icelanders to tame a hostile land, slower numbers having an ethereal quality, reminiscent of drifting ice.

# Eating & Drinking

The Icelanders are conservative eaters. As most of their food has to be imported, they have picked up Western habits and tastes. Breakfast is as likely to be cereal and coffee in Iceland as it is elsewhere, but older Icelanders still eat more traditional foods. For breakfast they will have *súrmjólk*, a form of sour milk, which looks and tastes like thin, light yogurt; or

*Ristað brauð með osti*, hot toast served with butter, marmalade and thinly sliced Icelandic cheese.

For that important mid-morning snack to keep hunger pangs at bay, kiosks at bus stations and most bakeries sell rolls of exaggerated length and dubious content and cakes shaped like prehistoric ammonites. These huge buns are topped with sugar or a type of icing which is coloured either pink or dark brown.

> **66** Apart from the cheeks, the Icelanders do not eat cod. They consider it an ugly fish and they do not eat ugly things. **99**

Lunch is a sandwich or something equally light. The main meal of the day is eaten in the evening and for this fish and lamb are the favourites. Smoked lamb (*hangikjöt*) which has been hung over a lamb-dung fire is as close to the real flavour of the country as it is possible to get – it is said that the fire must be of lamb dung to give the taste an extra piquancy. This may be true. What is definitely true is that Icelandic lamb, smoked or not, is delicious.

Unusual fish dishes, such as cod cheeks, are tender and full of flavour. The Icelandic economy is virtually founded on cod, yet – apart from the cheeks – the Icelanders do not eat it. They consider it an ugly fish and they do not eat ugly things*. Haddock is the one

* Until the 1950s Icelandic fishermen threw back lobsters they caught as they were too ugly to keep.

they prefer, claiming it to be much better looking.

Fresh vegetables and fruit are shipped in all year round, though some vegetables, such as carrots, potatoes and cauliflowers, are grown locally.

> **It is possible to indulge in every kind of cuisine in Reykjavík. There is even a 'One Woman Vegetarian' restaurant.**

Eating out is a favourite pastime, but an expensive one. As in all cosmopolitan capital cities, it is possible to indulge in every kind of cuisine in Reykjavík – Italian, Indian, Chinese, Vietnamese. There is even a 'One Woman Vegetarian' restaurant. A spectacular place to eat is the Pearl. It sits on top of a giant hot water tank built to store volcanically heated water for the central heating systems of the city. The restaurant revolves, adding an extra dimension – indeed, several – to a meal. This is either unappetising or brilliant fun, depending upon your point of view, but since it is too expensive to eat there, it doesn't really make much odds.

## Soured seal flipper and pan-fried puffin

Viking delicacies such as rams' testicles pickled in whey, congealed blood pudding, shark meat putrefied by being buried in the ground for several months, seal flipper soured in a way best left undefined, and boiled and pressed sheep's head, are claimed to be original.

Icelanders wonder why the only authentic Viking restaurant in Reykjavík is not popular with visitors, while visitors wonder at the existence of even one.

Another Viking speciality can be found on the Westmann Islands. During the spring nesting season, the islanders collect puffins and puffin eggs. To collect the eggs, they throw themselves off the cliffs attached to thin ropes and swing about hundreds of feet above the lashing sea to reach the nests. Despite these antics having most clearly had their origins in hunger, the youth of the islands now practise the tradition as a sport, seeing who can travel the furthest, perform the most elegant arc, and survive. Adult puffins are netted on the cliff tops, an equally dangerous activity. Considering the effort involved, you would assume that puffin tastes like ambrosia. You would be mistaken. Pan-fried, boiled, braised or roasted – nothing can make the bird taste like anything other than used sump oil.

> 66 To collect the eggs, they throw themselves off the cliffs attached to thin ropes and swing about hundreds of feet above the lashing sea. 99

The country's financial woes have seen a resurgence of interest in their own unique dishes as Icelanders realise they are both cheap and nutritious. Puffin is not so popular as dried fish. All over Iceland, but particularly in the north, fish of all types are hung out to dry on huge fish-drying frames like clothes on a line.

They are left until they are as thin as paper and taste of old carpet. When the seagulls have lost interest in them, the Icelanders will begin to consider the fish ready to eat.

## Coffee with a kick

The traditional drink in Icelandic cafés is coffee which varies from just drinkable to lethal. Icelanders thrive on it, but visitors, especially those of a more delicate constitution, may find that two cups will bring on the shakes.

> **❝ The traditional drink in Icelandic cafés is coffee which varies from just drinkable to lethal. ❞**

Many older Icelanders do not add sugar to their coffee but instead keep a *sykurmoli* (sugarcube) in their mouths while they are drinking, a habit which could go some way to explaining the silence of coffee drinkers. Although the young are adopting the Western habit of putting sugar in the cup, the word lives on in *Sykurmolarnir* – The Sugarcubes – one of the island's most popular rock groups. Björk at one time was their lead singer.

## All kinds of alcohol

It is said that God's gift to the Icelanders was a virgin land of incomparable beauty and diversity. The price modern Icelanders have to pay for the gift is the cost of alcohol.

Until 1989 beer was banned and even now is only available at state-controlled outlets at extortionate prices. The idea that prohibition would reduce drunkenness flew in the face of both logic and experience. In common with those other Vikings in Norway and Sweden, the Icelander long ago sorted out the problem of the long, dark winter months. The solution was straightforward: get drunk in September and don't sober up until late April.

> 66 The Icelander long ago sorted out the problem of the dark winter months: get drunk in September and don't sober up until late April. 99

Under prohibition, alcohol was available at certain times and places, one of which was when you were airborne. This meant that drinking started as the aeroplane was taxiing to the end of the runway and stopped only when the doors opened at the flight's end. By then it was usually possible to pour the passengers out of the plane rather than have them disembark in the usual way.

Another effect of prohibition was that alcohol smuggling and illicit stills for bootleg drink were commonplace. The home-made version was so awful that large quantities of Coca-Cola had to be consumed to drown the taste. Habits die hard, and many older Icelanders still drink copious amounts of Coke, keeping the country's youth company.

Drinking is now legal, but controlled. Alcohol of any description can still only be bought at government liquor stores and is very expensive. It is permitted in restaurants and bars where it is even more expensive. Making alcohol more accessible has reduced the amount consumed, but has had no effect on the nature of drinking. Icelanders do not understand social drinking. They drink purely to get drunk, a condition they seek with maximum enthusiasm at minimum expense. If it costs 10% less to get drunk on gin than on whisky, they will drink gin. Enquire whether taste is a consideration and they will look at you as if you are a fool. What could taste have to do with it?

**❝ The only truly Icelandic drink, *brennivín* (made from potatoes), tastes of nothing, cuts the throat like liquid emery paper and is known, as 'black death'. ❞**

As if to prove the point, the only truly Icelandic drink, *brennivín* (made from potatoes), tastes of nothing, cuts the throat like liquid emery paper and is known, with very good reason, as 'black death'. The Icelandic slang expression for drinking is 'to have a tear': clearly the power of the brew has long made the eyes water.

The first of March is National Beer Day, celebrating the end of prohibition. The festivities take the form of a 24-hour-long binge largely indistinguishable from the celebrations on all other days.

# Health

## Life and death

Icelanders have the highest life expectancy of any country in the world other than people in (the ex-Soviet State of) Georgia who are said to live regularly to 125. The people put this down to their love of the outdoors – and there is an awful lot of outdoors to love – and their diet.

> **Most Icelanders are of the opinion that any pain is an inconvenience that will right itself in an hour or two, or a day at most.**

Not that long ago doctors were in short supply. The best help that could be obtained in country areas was the district nurse who was quite likely to be unavailable in spring because she was busy castrating that year's rams. A wise old family member would be all that was possible for consultation. As a result, most Icelanders are of the opinion that any ailment or pain is a minor problem, an inconvenience that will right itself in an hour or two, or a day at most. However, outside influences are putting this healthy aspect of Icelandic life into a new perspective. The young are beginning to believe that the rest of the world could well be right and that all minor ailments and pains are quite possibly to be symptomatic of something life threatening. Potions and pills are catching on.

Death is celebrated with a gathering of large numbers of family and friends. Though preferring to maintain their privacy most of the time, people come together for funerals in a spirit of warmth and fellow feeling.

Beautiful music and poetry form part of the ceremony at which the coffin is draped in the national flag. At the graveside, a poignant 16th-century psalm is sung about the life of man being as transitory as a little meadow flower which falls to the scythe:

> The sickle's blade descendeth
> Then in a moment's span
> Its bloom and beauty endeth
> So ends the life of man.

Death is becoming big business, people having realised that their funeral is the last possible status symbol. Increasingly, bands are hired to play the favourite music of the deceased and parties are organised. Absolved of all responsibility for the actions of the guests and the expense of it all, the corpses have the time of their lives.

## Doctors and dentists

The Icelanders claim that their high life expectancy is due in part to their excellent national health service. They pay a small fee when they go to a doctor, a bigger one to see a specialist.

The health service does not extend to dentists. This is understandable considering the quantity of sweets consumed by Icelanders of all ages. There is no insurance cover available for dentistry either. It is quite simple: you eat sweets, you get bad teeth, you go to the dentist and afterwards you settle his bill. The

> **Despite all the sugar in their diet, the Icelanders are rarely obliged to fork out for fillings.**

pain might be in your mouth, but you will certainly pay through the nose. The redeeming feature of this financial consideration is that it has promoted good oral hygiene so that, despite all the sugar in their diet, Icelanders are rarely obliged to fork out for fillings.

## Condoms from cabbies

Never having suffered from the puritanism of the Saxons, Icelanders fix their condom machines to the walls of bus stations rather than hiding them away in the 'Gents'. Even taxi drivers sell condoms. This is a sensible measure, though there is always the fear of the taxi driver demanding that one recites the first lines of *Njál's saga* before he parts with a packet.

The financial crisis of 2008 saw the price of condoms rise dramatically as stocks had to be imported and the kroner fell against all major currencies. Sales of condoms therefore reduced but, with typical Icelandic flair, this was seen as potentially useful. Since the country's debt might take generations to clear, it was no bad thing that there might be an increase in the population.

## Getting into hot water

Icelanders are both healthy and hygienic. The former they put down to the latter. Every town has an open-air swimming pool where all the year round people swim daily, the old folk early, the schoolchildren and parents later in the day. All are obliged to shower and wash before entering the water which is volcanically heated so that, in winter, when the ground is covered in snow and the wind is trying

**66 Each pot is painted a different shade of red to indicate the colour your body will become. 99**

to move the water from the deep end to the shallow end, the Icelanders will still be steadily doing laps. It is a strange sight, steam from the hot water adding a surreal touch as heads covered with frost bob relentlessly up and down.

Beside the pools steps go down into circular 'hot pots' in which bathers rest prior to and after swimming. The volcanic water varies from hot in the first pot to unbelievably hot in the last and each pot is painted a different shade of red to indicate the colour your body will become, from the first strength in pale pink to the last from which you will emerge as red as a lobster.

With all this showering and swimming Icelanders are very clean. The only slight drawback is that volcanic water smells of sulphur. It takes a while for outsiders to get used to the idea that very clean people can stink of rotten eggs.

> 66 Having no national rude gesture, the people have to content themselves with publicly humiliating those they wish to offend. 99

Hygiene even extends to the eco-system. Any outsider wishing to fish in Iceland requires a certificate to prove to Icelandic officials that anything he intends putting into the water (waders, fishing rods, flies, etc.) has been sterilised. So even the salmon remain 'in the pink'.

# Government & Bureaucracy

## Trading insults

Having no national rude gesture, Icelanders have to content themselves with publicly humiliating those they wish to offend. The greatest humiliations are reserved for their politicians, the very greatest for those who attain the highest offices. You can be sure that if a politician has an offensive nickname, he is someone who has been singled out for high office. If it is really offensive, he is probably the prime minister.

Being the first nation in the world to elect a woman

as head of state swells the national chest, but the people's attitude towards the position of president is in marked contrast to that afforded to other politicians. Since they view politics as the province of the stupid and corrupt, they hold all politicians in low esteem and every couple of years give them the opportunity of finding a decent way of earning a living by the straightforward expedient of kicking them out.

**66 They view politics as the province of the stupid and corrupt. 99**

Unfortunately some politicians were given directorships of the National Bank when they lost office, a fact that annoyed the voters who did not have that in mind at all. One irate Icelander referred to the National Bank as the kindergarten for unloved politicians. This caused great offence and, therefore, great amusement.

Newspapers reflect the nation's feeling about all politicians; in fact it is generally assumed that reporters are under an obligation to be insulting. However, the source of their ire is not that politicians are evil or lead immoral lives, but that they are inept and stupid. By contrast, those who are insulted by politicians are shocked. It is as though the ducks had started to shoot back. A television producer with a string of deeply offensive political shows to his credit was insulted – as he saw it – by a government minister. With cries of outrage, he declared his intention of supporting libel cases for those who found themselves in a similar position, and promptly formed the Association of People Who Have Been Insulted By Politicians.

## Left, right and centre

Iceland has 63 members of parliament drawn from a handful of main parties. The Independence Party, the party with the largest number of seats, held power in a moderately right-wing coalition with the Progressives for nearly a century, but there has been an amalgam of left-wing parties to form the Social Democratic Alliance which, with the growth of the Left-Green Movement, has altered the old order. The difference seemed, at first, to matter little to most of the populace

> **66 The financial crisis of 2008 made everyone rather more interested in politics, to the extent that crowds gathered to protest. 99**

who believe that differences between a useless right-wing government and a useless left-wing government are frequently overstated in other countries.

However, the global credit crunch, while reinforcing that view, made everyone rather more interested in politics to the extent that crowds gathered outside the Parliament building in Reykjavík to protest at the ineffectual way in which the government was handling the situation. Finding the politicians unwilling to meet with them, the protesters went home, grabbed kitchen utensils and returned to bang them so loudly that the government and civil service were forced to abandon their work because of the infernal racket. The threat that the noise would be repeated on a daily basis caused the government to fall. The event is now known as the Pots and Pans Revolution.

The off-beat way in which this protest was handled is typical of the people. When Icelandic women calculated that on average they were being paid only 64.1% of the men's income, they staged a demonstration timed to take place at 2.08 p.m. – precisely 64.1% of the way through the working day.

**66 A poll claimed that despite the leftward trend there were just three Communists in the country. 99**

Iceland's shift to the left is seen as truly significant. However, it is not a seismic shift: despite the leftward trend, a poll found that there were just three Communists in the country. One was the gum-chewing presenter of Iceland's best radio jazz programme. The second was the keeper of the most northerly lighthouse, a man known as Óli the Commie, who is rumoured to have a picture of Stalin on the wall. The third person was not named for fear of libel action.

## The uncivil civil service

The civil service, having been around for the same length of time as the coalition, looks more like the government than the government does. Its employees often behave that way too, subverting democracy by obstructing progress when they disagree with proposals of the elected members.

Even when the government has voted in favour of something it can sometimes be difficult to get it done. There will be some junior clerk in some obscure ministry who

> **"The Icelanders are strong believers in the existence of the *Kolkrabbi* (Octopus), an organisation who control most of the major businesses. "**

does not like the idea. Once he has halted progress, the whole stubborn machinery of the civil service will come in on his side and the idea will be lost in a welter of red tape. It's an attitude which leads to the suggestion that Iceland could successfully do away with a layer of government, namely the elected layer.

# Business

The Icelanders are strong believers in the existence of the *Kolkrabbi* (Octopus), an organisation (probably informal but, as always with these things, who knows?) of the country's leading families who control most of the major businesses and have members within the government. Historically a close association certainly seemed to exist between big business and the leading political party with politicians becoming spokesmen for the businesses, and directors of the leading banks (very high earners) being political appointees. A sighting of a politician and businessman together in a car is usually accompanied by sneering comments about meetings of the Octopus, though, as with all other political scandals, people much prefer sarcasm and insults to real action.

The Icelanders also believe that the next largest political party and another group of influential men (chiefly rich farmers) form the Squid. Depending on the composition of the current coalition, the Octopus and the Squid will either be at daggers drawn or enjoying cosy lunches to their mutual advantage. But whichever way it goes, you can be sure that the ordinary Icelander will derive little benefit.

**66 If the Taiwanese invented battery-operated back scratchers, by the end of the first week of production an Icelander would have formed a business to import them. 99**

A decade ago, behind the complaining about the activities of the Octopus, enterprising souls were striving to join the club. Success was not immediate. Many set up businesses, starting small and usually getting smaller before they disappeared. If the Taiwanese invented battery-operated back scratchers, you could rest assured that by the end of the first week of production an Icelander would have formed a business to import them. Money would be borrowed, premises hired and staff employed, but more often than not to no avail, the bottom having fallen out of the back scratcher market within two weeks. The government approved of all this commerce, one minister having been tempted to state that the number of bankruptcies in the country was a measure of its economic health. The remark suggested a patronising attitude of the elite to the attempts of the average man.

The remark seemed rather too close to a disastrous truth in 2008 when it looked like the country itself might go bankrupt after the nation's three banks slid towards insolvency. To the rest of the world things looked very bad, but the Icelanders seemed to take the financial disaster in their stride. The fishing industry was still there, the possibilities for selling green geo-thermal energy were still good, and the increasing need for data centres and data storage facilities looked set to make Iceland the top 'hotspot' since it can offer inexpensive sustainable resources, plus limitless natural chill.

**❝ To the rest of the world things looked very bad, but the Icelanders seemed to take the financial disaster in their stride. ❞**

Iceland might have to borrow less, and the great adventure of buying the world – it seemed at one time to own half the British High Street (including Hamleys, Oasis and Whistles) as well as several football teams – would have to be put on hold, but the resourceful Icelanders are used to learning from their mistakes. They retained their faith in their own abilities – a faith apparently without limits. Some individuals with large debts to foreign banks or companies lost a great deal, including their houses. But for many, the crisis was just another storm to be weathered. It even brought its own (albeit gallows) humour:

"What is the capital of Iceland?"

"About $50."

# Custom & Tradition

## Sons and dóttirs

The majority of Icelandic Christian names are as old as the sagas. There you find Harald of the Grey Cape and Bork Blue Tooth Beard.

**66 Today it is possible to have a drink with Stone, son of Wolf (Steinn Úlfsson), or with Eagle, son of Bear (Örn Björnsson). 99**

Today it is possible to have a drink with Stone, son of Wolf (Steinn Úlfsson), or with Eagle, son of Bear (Örn Björnsson). And, what is more, it is possible to do so without having your head cleaved in twain and your wife broached.

Icelanders take great pride in being the only Viking country to maintain patronyms, the use of the father's given name as the child's surname. The usage pro-

78

duces the oddity of a standard family of father, mother, son and daughter having four different surnames. If Pétur, the son of Björn, marries Guðrún, daughter of Vilhjálmur, and they have two children, Marta and Einar, at a European hotel the family will sign in as Pétur Björnsson, Guðrún Vilhjálmsdóttir, Marta Pétursdóttir and Einar Pétursson. Hotel receptionists have been known to weep.

The use of patronyms has the potential to make the telephone directory one of the most difficult books in the world to follow. To counter the problem, it lists everybody

> **❝The use of patronyms has the potential to make the telephone directory one of the most difficult books in the world to follow. ❞**

by both Christian and surnames. But this is only a partial solution as there is a limited number of Christian names so there are always several people with the same names. So here the Icelanders add the profession of the person. Only then is the address given. Almost as an afterthought the telephone number is listed, although by the time they have waded through all the earlier information most folk have forgotten why they wanted to make the call.

The number of European-style surnames is now increasing as immigrants settle and Icelanders marry outsiders. One person who dropped his patronym for the European form a long time ago was the author Halldór Laxness. In anyone else this would be looked

down on as an affectation. In his case it was accept-
able because he is looked upon as a genius.

## Spring hop

The earliest Icelanders had a miserable time during the
five months of winter, even more miserable than their
modern compatriots. To keep themselves sane they
had regular festivals, the most important being the
midwinter *þorrablót* named after the ancient Norse
month of *Þorri*. This began with feasting during the
third week of January, and by the time the celebrations were over in the third
week of February, the days
were rapidly getting longer,
and spring was on its way.

It became customary for
Icelanders to welcome *Þorri*
by putting only one leg into
their trousers and hopping barefoot around the yard.
The church authorities tried to end the festival (not
least, perhaps, to avoid half Iceland's congregations
hobbling into church on crutches as a result of a single
frost-bitten foot), but it was revived under Danish rule
as a symbol of nationalism. Today it is enthusiastically
celebrated for much the same reason that the earliest
settlers enjoyed it. Traditional foods are eaten and a
quantity of drink consumed. The hopping is no longer
compulsory, but is quite likely to occur at those gath-

> **It became customary for Icelanders to welcome Þorri by putting only one leg into their trousers and hopping barefoot around the yard.**

erings where sufficient lubrication has been provided to remove all inhibitions.

## Rash Wednesday

In a festival that mixes the pagan past and the Christian present, on Ash Wednesday all Icelandic children put on fancy dress and spend the day trying to humiliate adults.

Quite the weirdest aspect of the festival is *kattarslagur* in which the children use home-made swords or clubs to sever a rope suspended through a

> 66 On Ash Wednesday all Icelandic children put on fancy dress and spend the day trying to humiliate adults. 99

barrel. Not so long ago, for reasons lost in the mists of time, a dead cat was hung on the end of the rope. Nowadays, to the relief of all concerned, and most especially the Icelandic cat population, a fluffy toy hangs from the rope.

Ash Wednesday is preceded by Bun Day, the Icelandic equivalent of Shrove Tuesday. This sounds normal enough, but even this Icelandic festival includes the bizarre, the custom being to win a bun for having hit someone across the backside with a stick before he or she has got out of bed.

## The need to knit

Thirty years ago knitting would have rated a score as high on the national obsession scale as politics and the weather. In country areas it still does, but the town dwellers have long since stopped indulging in what they perceive as a yokel's pursuit, in public at least. Many of Iceland's excellent young artists are women who have put down their knitting needles and taken up paint brushes.

Both men and women knitted. They made blankets from knitted triangles, gloves with fingers but without seams (a skill which still attracts the admiration of the knowledgeable), sweaters, anything and everything to keep out winter's chills. Stories of obsessional knitting are legion. Cow and sheep herders knitted as they walked across Iceland's rugged landscape. Farmers' wives were even said to have knitted while they made love.

> **❝ Many of Iceland's excellent young artists are women who have put down their knitting needles and taken up paint brushes. ❞**

A beautiful product of all this endeavour is the *lopi,* the sweater with the characteristic half-moon of intricate patterning around the neck. Those made for sale to visitors tend to be made with the addition of soft imported wool, because the wool from Icelandic sheep (which have long guard hairs to keep out winter's chills) is coarse. The Icelanders call articles knitted from it *stingubolur,* literally 'underwear that pierces', because it is so prickly.

# Language & Ideas

The Dane, Rasmus Christian Rask, claimed in the early 19th century that he had learned Icelandic in order to be able to think. This was a wonderful, some would even say moving, compliment. But he also predicted that Icelandic would be dead in 100 years, killed off by Danish, the language of the island's rulers. The rulers did not ban Icelandic (merely ignored it) and the language survived.

> **It is ironic that the working man's dislike of the upper class saved the language from extinction.**

Danish was the language of commerce and government. It was also the language of snobbery, used by the Icelandic 'gentry'. It is ironic that the Icelanders' dislike of pretension and the working man's dislike of the upper class saved the language from extinction.

Similar predictions are now being made about the death of Icelandic at the hands of English. The particular problem is the number of English-speakers who come to Iceland to study, drawn by its uniqueness. If a class has ten Icelanders and one non-Icelandic-speaking foreigner then the lecture will be given in English. The Icelanders have a term for this – 'Ignorance is Strength' – which illuminates their concern for their language.

To the list of obsessions another could have been

added – Icelandic. Icelandic is an exotic language based on an alphabet with 33 letters, the extra ones being extremely picturesque and completely unpronounceable. A poem in Icelandic by William Jón Holm entitled The Icelandic Language, expresses it thus:

> In an airconditioned room you cannot understand
>     the grammar of this language,
> The whirring machine drowns out the soft vowels,
> But you can hear these vowels in the mountain wind
> And in heavy seas breaking over the hull of a small
>     boat.
> Old ladies can wind their long hair in this language
> And can hum, and knit, and make pancakes.
> But you cannot have a cocktail party in this
>     language
> And say witty things standing up with a drink in
>     your hand.
> You must sit down to speak this language,
> It is so heavy you can't be polite or chatter in it.
> For once you have begun a sentence, the whole
>     course of your life is laid out before you,
> Every foolish mistake is clear, every failure, every
>     grief,
> Moving around the inflections from case to case
>     and gender to gender,
> The vowels changing and darkening, the consonants
>     softening on the tongue

Till they are the sound of a gull's wings fluttering
As he flies out of the wake of a small boat drifting
    out to open water.

Most Icelanders are as proud of their language as
they are of their country and protect it fiercely from
what they view as external invasion. Committees set
up for its protection go to great lengths to avoid
absorbing foreign words, and when a new concept or
invention is imported into Iceland, set about produc-
ing an Icelandic equivalent. The
sagas are scoured for a word no
longer in common usage that
can be pressed into service. To
avoid 'telephone' the word *sími*

> **66 To avoid 'telephone' the word *sími* was dredged up, an ancient word for a thread. 99**

was dredged up, an ancient word for a thread.
'Satellite' – *gervitungl* – was tricky, but was manufac-
tured from the words for 'artificial' and 'moon'.
Television is *sjónvarp*, combining the words for seeing
and casting out (as in fishing), while computer com-
bines *tala* – the word for number – and *völva* – sooth-
sayer or prophetess – to create *tölva*. Despite the con-
cocted nature of these words and the Icelanders' love
of the very latest technology, they are readily accepted
and used by everyone.

Very occasionally something comes along that creates a real problem: what to do, for instance, with
'inter-continental ballistic missile'? The sagas did not

offer a word for 'spear thrown from a great distance' so a new one had to be made up which means 'long distance fiery flying thing'. Most Icelanders say ICBM. To the concern of older folk the young seem more willing to assimilate words from other languages, chiefly English, again raising the fear that a language with such a small number of users is under threat.

> **It is likely that berserkers were totally intoxicated, a condition much favoured by the population.**

No Icelandic words inhabit the international lexicon, though the Icelanders do lay claim to several of Viking origin that have found their way into English. Best of all they like *berserk*, probably deriving from 'bear-skin' and used as a term for warriors who fought with the strength of ten men and were immune to pain. It is likely that berserkers were totally intoxicated, a condition much favoured by the population.

The Icelanders are pleased to the point of embarrassment if a foreigner learns their language. At one time it was discovered that a Georgian lawyer had taught himself Icelandic. He did not know any Icelanders and had done it purely for his own enjoyment, translating a quantity of Icelandic literature into his own language. The Icelanders were so impressed and grateful, they invited the man and his wife to Iceland at the country's expense, and wined and dined them for the entire two months.

# The Author

Richard Sale was born in England's West Country – reason enough to feel sympathy with all minorities who speak with strange tongues.

Being quite good at sums he took a degree in theoretical physics and a PhD in astrophysics, and then sought a job in glaciology in order to be nearer his first great loves, snow and ice. He is now a travel writer, specialising in wilderness areas, most particularly the Arctic.

He fell in love with Iceland the first time he saw it – barely, through the fine rain that was falling – and has been going there, summer and winter, ever since. He is constantly frustrated by its weather and endlessly fascinated by its mixture of landscapes, its bird life and its people (though not always in that order). Happily, the elements and birds combined to win him and co-author Eugene Potapov the prestigious US Wildlife Society's Book of the Year Award for their work, *The Gyrfalcon* – the white Arctic falcon, the world's biggest.

He would like to thank several Icelandic friends for their (sometimes inadvertent) assistance with this guide. Sadly, none of them is willing to be identified.

### The Greeks

The Greeks exhibit an extreme passion for freedom of choice – which has turned law circumvention into an art, and has made them incapable of comprehending words like 'discipline', 'co-ordination' or 'system'.

### The Canadians

Canadians have been heard to claim that the Canadian flag is the most popular flag in the world. Why? Because it has a bar at each end. A strategy like this appeals even to the 'hosers' (lager louts) in Quebec.

### The Danes

Danes co-operate. LEGO comes from the Danish words *leg godt* which mean 'play well', and this is just what the Danes are good at. In any brochure the word 'co-operation' will appear at least three times per page along with a generous sprinkling of 'joint ventures'.

### The Americans

The American language embraces the bias towards good feelings. Stocks that plummet to half their value aren't losers, they're 'non-performers'. Someone doesn't have a near brush with death; he or she has a 'life-affirming experience'.

### The Spanish

Anyone attempting to understand the Spanish must first of all recognise the fact that they do not consider anything important except total enjoyment. If it is not enjoyable it will be ignored.

### The English

The English share a dislike of anyone behaving in a manner that 'goes too far'. The admired way to behave in almost all situations is to display a languid indifference. Even in affairs of the heart, it is considered unseemly to show too much enthusiasm.

Comments on other titles

On the series:

"If I were a cabaret artist or stand up comedian, I'd just get up and read these books to the audience as they would bring the house down."   Reviewer of *Het Parool*, Holland

The Swedes:

"Funny and true portrait of the Swedes. Arm yourself with this book before you meet Inga and Sven. Very very funny — don't go to Sweden without it!"   Reader from England

The Scots:

"A sympathetic (but not unquestioning), highly entertaining look at what makes the Scots tick."   Scots reader from Ireland

The Italians:

"A book you just can't refuse. Hilarious insights into the Italian man and the mother behind him."   Reader from San Francisco

The Germans:

"The nature of the Germans — very funny but true description. You must read this book if you want to learn more about the strange nature of the Germans, because you will find it in no other."   German reader from Stuttgart

# Xenophobe's®
## guides

# Xenophobe's®
## lingo learners

66 Speak the lingo by speaking English. 99

(O)

# Oval Books

5 St John's Buildings Canterbury Crescent London SW9 7QH

The Xenophobe's® Guide series can be bought via Amazon or from **Oval Books** by contacting us directly, or through our web site:

www.ovalbooks.com

Oval Books
5 St John's Buildings
Canterbury Crescent
London SW9 7QH

Payment can be made by cheque (payable to Oval Books), or by credit card*

telephone: +44 (0)20 7733 8585
e-mail: info@ovalbooks.com

**Oval Books** charges the full cover price for its books (because they're worth it) and £2.00 for postage and packing, but for more than one book (to one address) postage and packing will be FREE.

Xenophobe's® Guides are also available as e-books. Please refer to our web site:

www.ovalbooks.com

*We accept Visa or Mastercard. Orders are dispatched as soon as the card details and mailing address are received. If the mailing address is not the same as the card holder's address it is necessary to give both.

$\bigcirc$
Oval Books